Figure fifty-four: Selected place names.

BRAMLEY
HALF A CENTURY OF CHANGE

ANTHONY SILSON

Hobson's Yard about thirty years ago. Offices now occupy the area.

'To My Mother: A life-long Bramley resident'

The photograph on the front cover shows Simpson's Farm about 1955.

The photograph on the back cover shows the view from about the same position today.

Published by the Author at Leeds LS13 2HZ
First published 1991
Copyright Anthony Silson, 1991
All rights reserved. No part of this publication may be reproduced, stored in a retrieval system, or transmitted, in any form or by any means, electronic, mechanical, photocopying, recording or otherwise, without the prior permission of the publisher.

ISBN 0 9517895 0 3

Printed by Allanwood Press, Town Street, Stanningley, Pudsey, Leeds LS28 6EZ

Introduction

Britain entered into war with Germany in 1939. A year or two before E.T. Carr wrote two books: *The Lands of Bram* and *Industry in Bramley*. Now, some fifty or so years after the near coincidence of these two events, one national and one parochial, seems a good time to review the enormous changes that have affected Bramley over that time. Some will see these changes as progress; some will regret them and see in them the destruction of a community; but all must surely agree that Bramley is now a very different place to what it was when we went to war.

Since Carr's works were published other excellent books on Bramley, including *The Village That Disappeared* and *Bramley Bygones* have been published. None, though, of these more recent works, seem to examine the recent spatial changes in Bramley as a whole and it is particularly this deficiency that I have sought to rectify in this work.

My sources have included books on Bramley, directories, old Council documents, newspapers, magazines, photographs, maps and memories. Field work has been an important source, especially on Bramley as it is today. Most of the fieldwork was carried out in the early part of 1989.

The statistical material presented depends not only on the accuracy of the sources but on my perception as to where the boundaries of Bramley are to be placed and my decisions as to where to allocate certain borderline activities in the classification used. Whilst any errors are my responsibility, throughout my work I have done my best to present an account that is as accurate as possible. And I have done my best to captivate your interest on a topic that has been a pleasure to write.

To the staff of Bramley Library and the History Room, Leeds Reference Library and to all the other people who have in any way helped me in my task, I offer my sincere thanks. I am particularly grateful for the permission granted by Leeds City Libraries to reproduce figures, 5, 9, 17, 20, 38 for the approval of Leeds Education Department to reproduce, from the author's collection, figures 1, 2 and 21 and for the loan of treasured photographs from Mr J. Bennett for figure 4 and Mrs E. Spurr for figure 6. All the remaining photographs are either from the author's collection (figures 3 and 16) or are taken by the author.

Before the War

In 1937 an unknown chronicler wrote "old timers still cling to the title 'Our Village', but I am afraid that Bramley can no longer be so designated." This opinion was by no means without foundation. Even at that time Bramley was larger, perhaps, than a village should be, had more services, perhaps, than a village should possess. Yet if it was not exactly a village, many of its buildings were set amongst farmland, it had character, even if the most well disposed person could scarcely call it pretty, and its residents felt some identity with it and each other.

Former fields and bygone buildings, surely it is these which first spring to mind when we think of old Bramley and it is the narration of developments in the landscape that forms the core of this work. But the community has changed too and so our story begins with a glimpse of some of the varied social activities that took place before the war.

Bramley celebrated the Coronation of King George VI with some style to say the least. For some years previous to the Coronation, Bramley Park had been enhanced by a fine bandstand. It was replaced as part of the Coronation celebrations, by a small house built, and furnished, by local schoolchildren. With hindsight, their considerable effort seems misplaced for the Coronation Villa was soon vandalised and the site is now a play area. The Coronation celebrations began on Tuesday evening and were not concluded until the following Sunday evening. The very varied programme included concerts, dancing, several sporting activities, a sheep dog trials and a best decorated house competition.

Such a programme took some organising but Bramley people were by no means without experience in running large scale events. A carnival was held annually and only a couple of years before the Coronation, a Joy Week had successfully raised funds for Leeds Infirmary. Joy Week's joint organisers were Mr Lawson, a local garage owner, and Mr Sweetman, the Headteacher of Bramley National School (figure one).

Evidently large scale events brought together many sections of Bramley's society. The Coronation Celebrations' Committee included Councillor Haley (President), the Reverend Womersley (Chairman), Mr Lawson (Vice Chairman) and Mr Sweetman (a committee member).

Bramley's schools were not only prominent in major events but were at least equally, if not more, significant in promoting Bramley's day to day social life. There were, before the war, two small schools, Christ the King and Good Shepherd, and three large schools, Broad

Figure one: Bramley National teachers, 1946
Back row: Pickles, Smith, Pointon, Benson, Reed, Kinder, Morris, Barrett, Cook.
Front row: Webster, uncertain, Greaves, Sweetman, Wilkinson, Tolson, Goldthorpe, uncertain.

Lane, Hough Lane and Bramley National (see figure forty-two). Once enrolled at one of these latter schools, a child would almost always remain there until the legal leaving age was attained. In itself this helped some youngsters to know each other, even before they started work, but the schools also paved the way for social activities when the youngsters left school, (figure two).

At the risk of annoying some, but hopefully of pleasing others, we admit to a belief that Bramley National was particularly effective in promoting people's sense of identity with Bramley. After all it was scholars of this school who gathered the material for two books on Bramley and it was a teacher at the school, E.T. Carr, who compiled this information into book form. Before the war it was usual for Bramley's teachers to live near the school where they taught and this, too, promoted a sense of community. Mr Greaves (see figure one) was one such teacher at Bramley National. As well as teaching there, he organised a schoolboys rugby team and played a prominent part in initially forming, and then supporting, Bramley Old Boys Rugby Club. So, through the efforts of people such as Mr Greaves, it was possible to progress from school rugby to that of Bramley Old Boys. Extra-curricular work, such as this, was achieved without the school in any way sacrificing academic achievement. Indeed, often pupils reached standards in literacy that many might well envy today.

If the schools laid the foundation for Bramley's social life, the several churches built upon these foundations by providing a large range of activities. Occasionally there were processions through the streets thereby bearing witness to the presence of the Church in Bramley. Some of those who, at school, had come to enjoy cricket might, as youngsters and young adults, continue to play by joining the cricket team of either Brunswick, or Moriah, Methodist Church. As a recreational centre, Moriah went further than the others by claiming to be the "Pioneers of Healthy Recreation for Young People". Whether or not this claim was justified, Moriah certainly did its members proud by offering, in addition to cricket, billiards, table tennis, draughts, dominoes and chess. Zion Baptist, whilst also offering several of these, was distinctive in being able to provide lawn tennis.

The City Council provided outdoor recreational facilities in Bramley Park and indoor facilities at the Baths where there was swimming in the summer and dancing in the winter.

Figure two: Senior boys of Broad Lane School, 1925

Figure three: Brunswick cricket field. Probably a Sunday School activity.

Figure four: Brunswick Cricket Team, 1937

At any season, and provided the projector did not break down, which it was wont to do, an engrossing hour or two could be passed watching the latest romance or comedy currently being shown at the Lido Cinema.

Figure five: The Lido Cinema, 1937

In a poem called The Good Old Days, written by Hilda Myers (and published in the Bramley Almanac, 1940) there is a character called Bill who states:

> "I loved to sit an' rest,
> On't top a Yonder Reservoir,
> An' watch t' sun sink in't west."

And like the imaginary Bill, there were plenty of real people who would enjoy a quiet few moments in the fields and byways of Bramley.

Enough has been said to show that residents, whether as individuals or as a group, could pursue so many enjoyable activities in Bramley that there was little need to travel further afield in search of recreational opportunity. The danger is obvious: people ran the risk of becoming too inward looking. The result is equally plain: residents identity with Bramley was enhanced.

It would be wrong though to leave an impression that life was all fun before the war. Far from it. Housework was harder than today.

Several houses had coal fired ovens which shone only through the vigorous application of black lead. In those homes which had not yet acquired gas boilers, garments were washed by first boiling them in a set pot. They were then dumped in a dolly tub and possered, before being wrung out in a hand worked wringing machine. Clothes were dried on a line strung out across the street, if the day were fine. If not, they were dried on a clothes horse before the open fire. Monday was wash day and, on a Monday, the smell of washing and steaming clothes, blending with the smell of simmering broth, made from the left overs of the weekend joint, wafts down the years.

Times, especially in the depression years, were often hard. Most youngsters began work at an age when many of today's teenagers have scarcely started their high school career. Hours of work were long and working conditions left something to be desired: at one clothing factory, rats not infrequently scurried by the workers' feet. Somewhat surprisingly, two of the three City Councillors were Conservative. Perhaps the inhabitants of the several large houses in Bramley voted Conservative. But votes must also have come from poorer people and this circumstance might have arisen from a belief

Figure six: Willie Spurr and his son, Harold, stand outside the Well House at the bottom of Warrel's Road. Water was, at one time, pumped from the well and then flowed downhill to Waterloo Mill.

amongst some who, whilst financially were rather poor, yet considered themselves to be a cut above the rest socially.

Whatever the niceties of social class, through often going to the same school, and through often working and playing together in Bramley, many people knew each other. Amongst the well-known were Mr W. and Mr H. Spurr. Both worked in the leather trade, an industry once well represented in Bramley. Both were of that breed of highly skilled craftsmen which even then was becoming rare. Anyone who ever had a pair of shoes repaired by Mr Harold Spurr will testify to the incredible high quality of his work.

Even before the war, the Well House, where the Spurrs had worked, had been demolished and replaced by a red-brick semi-detached house. New housing was already beginning to decimate Bramley's open spaces. Inevitably people, including H. Myers in the poem quoted earlier, were speaking of the good old days. For all that, pre-war changes were as nothing compared with the devastating changes that were to engulf Bramley in later years. But before these came to be fully realised Bramley people, like so many others, had to endure yet another world war.

The War Years

Many children show a keen interest in the place where they live. For such children war-time Bramley offered much to stimulate their senses. Fascinating smells wafted from the piggeries behind the public library or from the tanning of leather at Gibson's Hough End works. Within a weaving shed the smell of whitewashed walls blending with oil was combined with a ceaseless clatter as looms wove wool into cloth.

Above all, though, there was so much to watch, so much to see. As T.H. Wilson's workers shaped aluminium, little flashes of bright

Figure seven: Part of a ginnel, bounded by tall stone walls near Town Street, c.1962. The iron posts are to prevent cattle wandering down the ginnel.

white light lit up the nearby part of Town Street and, across the road, there was the red glow from the little furnace used by the blacksmith to shoe horses. Yet only a short distance away, Simpson's farm brought a sharply contrasted scene. There, at the right time, cows could be watched crossing the ginnel (figure seven) on their way to be milked. Down Ducky, too, cows might be watched grazing, especially at a moment when a train was not expected to steam by on the nearby railway. A short distance away, on the down platform at Bramley station, there was the little thrill to be felt as the wooden shelter shook when the "Lanky" sped westward. There were not only the expresses to excite but there was a wealth of detail to observe (figure eight). Former Great Northern semaphores swivelled up and down, and,

Figure eight: Bramley station c.1965. A somersault signal stands near the water tank. The building on the right is Turner Tanning.

sometimes, points clanged as coal trains shunted into the coal yards behind the main station buildings. There were points, but for a different purpose, at Town End. There, tram conductors could be watched switching the lines to enable trams to enter or leave the large tram shed, (figure nine).

All this diversity of activity was reflected in an equally diverse and complex landscape. In 1834 the main built up area was located along Town Street but several buildings were to be found along Broad Lane

15

Figure nine: Trams and, on the left, the tram shed at Bramley Town End. The white bands, painted on the lamp posts, are to aid visibility in the black out.

and some on Back Lane. Whilst at that time there were scarcely any other buildings, it is yet possible to consider that area, bounded today by lines linking Bramley station, Broad Lane School, St. Catherine's Mill and Town End, within which most of the few buildings then lay, to be the heart of Bramley. By 1914 part of the heart, especially in the Warrel's and Hough Lane areas, had become built up. Just before the outbreak of the Second World War, council estates in the Fairfields and at Sandford and a private estate in the Calverleys had not only substantially increased the built up area but had initiated large scale building outside the heart. Nevertheless large parts of Bramley still had a rural aspect in 1939 (figure twenty-four). Some agricultural land was trapped within the built up parts of the heart, a fact contributing to the rapid shifts of scene that so characterised Bramley. Most, though, of the farmed land formed an irregular zone surrounding the heart.

Bramley, in 1939, had its pig and poultry keepers but the two main farming enterprises were rhubarb growing and dairying. Even though some rhubarb fields almost reached Lower Town Street, most, with their distinctive dark, dwarfed and elongated sheds, were to be found slightly away from the heart of Bramley. Conversely, within and close to the heart, dairying was common. It is possible to read into this pattern the influence of different markets. Bramley residents drank the milk produced so there was some advantage in locating dairying near the houses but much of the rhubarb was sold in distant places, some as far afield as London, so there was no particular need to grow rhubarb especially close to houses.

Not all the food produced was for sale. Some folk spent their spare time tending an allotment or rearing poultry in places such as parts of the Warrel's and a long abandoned quarry near Stanningley Road. Such hobbies were to gain in significance as war-time food shortages grew. Other outdoor activities led, as they still do today, to open land at Barley Mow, Bramley Park and Bramley Fall Woods. As significant providers of outdoor recreation Brunswick and Moriah chapels each had a cricket field, one located slightly west of Bell Lane and the other adjacent to Bell Lane. Zion Baptist had tennis courts and a small plot of land on which Sunday School sports were held. Most of the remaining open land was associated with quarrying. Near the reservoir, former quarrying had left a deep craggy basin whilst at Newlay, in the north, and Park Spring, in the south, quarrying was still changing the face of the land.

Together, quarries, woods, crops and grass occupied most of Bramley but their associated activities employed few people. Instead most people worked in manufacturing and services. Some folk travelled to Leeds, or further still to Keighley, to their work but many found jobs within Bramley. For if, at that time, Britain still seemed to be one of the great workshops of the world, Bramley must have seemed to have had a goodly share of the British workshop. Bricks and jam, furniture and soap, organs and refrigerators, all these and many more were made in Bramley. But the textile industry was the most important. Stanningley Road including the area by the LNER railway, Town Street, Broad Lane and an area by the canal were the main places where factories were to be found but the overall pattern was a scattered one with, not uncommonly, factories found in the midst of houses and service industries.

For its size Bramley had an astonishing number of shops. A few were scarcely more than the living room of a house and it was these shops, along with several corner shops and small parades of shops in the council estates, that led to a scattering of shops throughout the built up area. The location of fish and chip shops (figure ten) well exemplifies the overall pattern. There were though, other types of shops, of which butchers is one example (figure eleven), which were much more strongly localised, especially along Town Street.

Table one shows that nearly two thirds of the shops were located in Stanningley Road and Town Street and that Town Street alone had

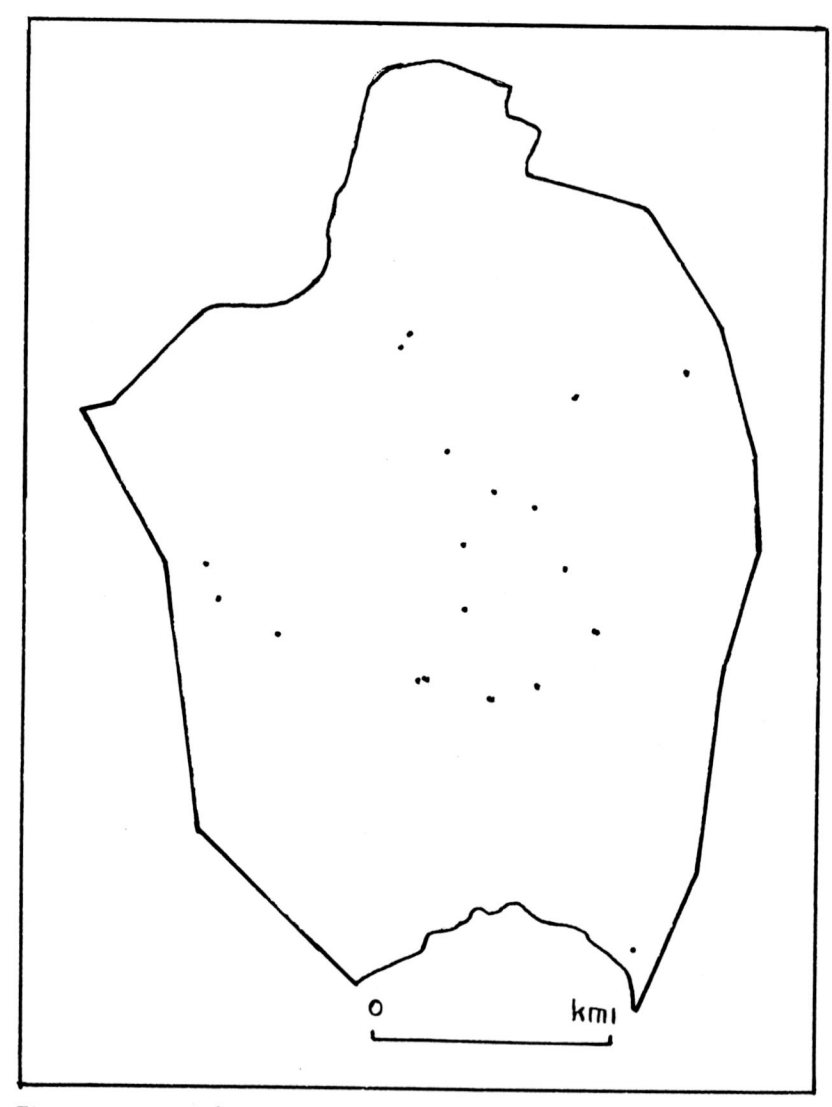

Figure ten: Distribution of Fish and Chip Shops, 1939.

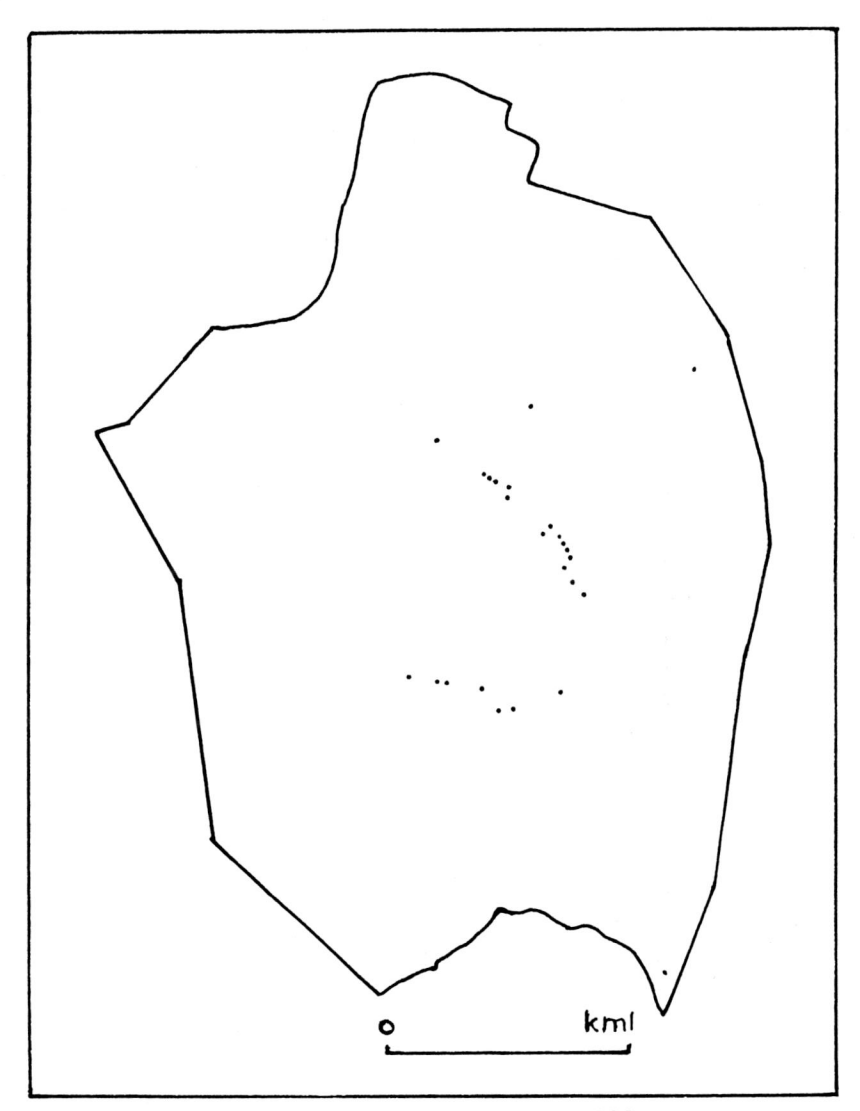

Figure eleven: Distribution of Butchers Shops, 1939.

Table One
Distribution of Shops in Bramley in 1939

Number of Shops Located in

	Town Street	Stanningley Road	Rest of Bramley	Total
Butchers and Greengrocers	25	8	7	40
Other Food Shops	39	17	47	103
Post Offices & Newsagents	4	2	13	19
Clothes and Footwear	17	6	8	31
Other Shops	17	4	3	24
Total	102	37	78	217

nearly one half of the total. It was here that most butchers, greengrocers, clothes and footwear and durable goods shops were to be found.

Only an extremely large scale map could adequately illustrate the complexity that was Town Street in 1939. But most of the manufacturing was located between Outgang and Highfield Road and the greatest number of shops lay between Outgang and Westover Road, with that part between Hough Lane and Westover Road particularly significant (table two).

Table Two
Number of Shops in Different Parts of Town Street in 1939

Broad Lane to Westover Road	Westover Road to Hough Lane	Hough Lane to Outgang	Outgang to Highfield Road	Highfield Road to Town End
12	38	29	18	5

(The five sections are of approximately equal length)

No part, though, was entirely without shops and other services and most parts had several houses. Most, but not all, of the buildings were made of stone that had become blackened with age. Often the buildings had slightly different designs and as their heights varied slightly the skyline was uneven (figure twelve). Town Street bends slightly so the whole cannot be seen at once and this characteristic, along with its diversity of land use and building types made it a remarkably interesting street to explore.

Figure twelve: Town Street from Raynville Road, 1960. The fields were later to become a housing estate. Notice the uneven skyline.

Figure thirteen: Raynville's landscapes today.

Figure fourteen: Vacant house and shop located on Town Street, opposite Moorfields, c.1962. Brick built flat roofed shops and flats now occupy the site.

And if trekking through Bramley had brought on a thirst, there were not only plenty of shops with soft drinks for sale – at least when the war started – but, for those of age, an abundance of public houses. Or if, instead, there was a need to sole and heel shoes, then there would be no difficulty in finding a cobblers as there were some twenty to choose from! Less fortunate, perhaps, were those who needed cash. There were only four banks, one on Stanningley Road, the rest near the junction of Town Street, Waterloo Lane and Hough Lane. So, like shops, some non-retailing services were concentrated but, overall, non-retailing services were scattered throughout the built up area. A wide range of goods could be bought in Bramley's shops and a wide range of non-retailing services were available. These included several churches and chapels, one private and one public library, the Baths, schools, two launderies, dressmakers and even a corsetiere!

Figure fifteen: Houses located near the Unicorn public house c.1962. The site is now open land.

The threat and reality of the war brought new sounds, new sights. New detail was added to the landscape with the building of a static water tank in Hough Lane and several air raid shelters. Bramley National School had one and dark, dank and dismal it was. Such features were mostly short-lived, though one shelter survived until 1985 and iron railings that were taken for salvage from garden walls have not been replaced.

Many homes experienced the anguish of a loved one called up for active service and later, some homes were saddened by the irreperable loss of one who would never return.

Those who were not called-up plunged with vigour into the war effort. Many followed a day's work with a night's fire watching. Some served in the Home Guard or as air raid wardens and many contributed to National Savings and a Spitfire fund. Yet, in mid 1941, at a critical period in the war, with the USSR recently invaded, Bramley folk were still able to relax. Zion Baptist had celebrated its Anniversary, Bramley Working Men's Club had beaten Stanningley Park at bowls and

Figure sixteen: Women played a key role in the war. Those with husbands away in the Armed Forces had to bring up children on their own. Women also worked in factories and service industries. This photograph, taken about 1941, also shows a gas lamp. Such lamps were still to be found in the quieter streets.

Moriah Methodist had won both its home and away cricket matches.

Much spare time was passed listening to the wireless and in regular visits to Bramley's two cinemas one of which, the Lido, was located in central Town Street. But the place to be seen was the recently opened Clifton, its initial centred above the screen, located at Town End. Homeward bound the place to scurry past was the Old Hall (figure eighteen). On a clear winter's night, with Town Street blacked out and

Figure seventeen: The Clifton Cinema in 1939. Just visible, in the background, is the telescopic chimney of Elmfield Mill.

Figure eighteen: The Old Hall in Lower Town Street c.1955.

a brilliant bomber's moon shining, it was only too easy to believe the tale of a man murdered in the Hall, of his bloodstain that no washing could remove and of his ghost that haunted the Hall. Equally easy to believe another tale told about Victoria Mill where, according to Greenwood Musgrave, "a watchman bold . . . old Jim Tiff" met an uncertain and untimely end.

A quite different mystery was how so many shop-keepers, who had eked out a living in peace-time, managed to survive at all in war-time. Grocers and butchers usually had something to sell because rationing brought equal shares of the necessities for everyone. Other shop-keepers often found supplies meagre at best and non-existent at worst. The record, though, for lack of stock must surely have been held by a corner shop at the junction of Grosmont Terrace and Grosmont Road. Perhaps more than anything else, the war brought shortages to Bramley folk. No surprise then that in one of its large advertisements in the Pudsey and Stanningley News, Jesse Stephenson should proudly announce that it had obtained new potatoes and tomatoes. Naturally, though, for registered customers only! No surprise either that in the later war years at the first meeting of the newly formed St. Peter's Youth Club a major item of business related to how tea and biscuits might be obtained. No, the surprise, in the war years, came when some **much wanted article was tracked down.** Nowadays post-war

Figure nineteen: Wartime shortage and restriction!

generations must find it hard to understand the pleasure felt when so mundane an object as a ruler could be bought, and harder still to appreciate the near ecstasy felt when a gramophone spring was tracked down or a shop – Chapman's to be precise – was discovered to have a pre-war stock of Hornby Train accessories. But for the most part it was a case of make do and mend. Almost anything was made at home, from the more obvious jams or soft drinks, to the less obvious briquettes built from coal dust. Many toys – such as that shown in figure nineteen – had perforce to be home made.

As might well be expected there were grumbles at the shortage of goods but there were only thanks that so few bombs fell. But some did, and, rare though they were, the raids by the Luftwaffe are not forgotten. That of August, 1942 was the worst. It was heralded by the dropping of flares which so brilliantly lit the sky that the streets were clearer than at full moon. The raid had begun before the alert sounded. This mattered little to the many residents who neither lived near a public shelter nor had a private shelter – not even a Morrison. Such people hoped for the best, the lonely moved into a neighbour's house for comfort and, from time to time, the more daring took a peep outside at what proved to be a noisy raid.

Bullets from machine guns whistled through the air. There were

Figure twenty: Bomb damage, Nansen Grove. This house, with its front on Nansen Avenue is mentioned in the text. The street shelter is unscathed from the raid.

27

tinkles of broken glass as windows shattered and dropped down. Mostly, though, the sounds were more thunderous as an occasional bomb burst and the anti-aircraft guns on Post Hill tried to blast the enemy from the skies.

An air raid shelter in the Nansens proved its worth to one family who, by sheltering there, escaped injury even though their nearby home was wrecked by a bomb. It was in this area, and another near Town End, that most bombs were dropped. Daylight then brought the inevitable small groups of sightseers inspecting the night's damage.

But in truth Bramley was not badly damaged by this, or any other raid. Even now, gratitude must be expressed that Bramley escaped so relatively lightly from so destructive a war. Moreover that so little damage was sustained is one fact of great significance in the development of Bramley's landscapes. It meant Bramley ended the war with mostly the same buildings as it possessed at the commencement of the war. The other significant facts are the war-time shortages and restrictions which meant scarcely any new buildings were constructed. Together they caused the landscape of Bramley to be scarcely altered during the war years.

Shortages continued into the immediate post-war years. Indeed, if

Figure twenty-one: Class J1A, Bramley National School, 1946. Elementary schools such as this continued into the immediate post-war years but a tripartite system (of modern, technical and grammar schools) would soon replace the elementary system.

anything, they increased and at no time was this more evident than in the winter of 1947. Children turned up for school but, the register having been taken, were then dismissed because there was no coke to heat the building. Not that homes were that much warmer, for at this time so many still relied on coal fires. The coincidence of a coal shortage with one of the severest winters of the century, when snow lay deep for days, made this a truly memorable winter. At the time it really did seem that winter would never end. It did, of course, and was followed by a hot summer. Not only did the seasons change, but, as the forties drew to a close, other changes were looming. Men and materials were becoming increasingly available and, in consequence, Bramley was to become dramatically transformed in the next thirty years.

The Years of Change

As if to compensate for that period of landscape stability occasioned by the war and its immediate aftermath, a spate of building swept across Bramley. The casualties were the farmers and market gardeners of Intake, Swinnow and the Ganners. Fields that, in the forties, had grown grass or rhubarb, had by the mid-fifties, been transformed into semi-detached houses and low flats frequently made of concrete (figure twenty-two). In these council estates the only growth, apart from that

Figure twenty-two: Concrete semi-detached houses, Intake.

in the small gardens, seemed to be the television aerials that eventually sprang up on virtually every chimney. The opening of a transmitter at Holme Moss in 1951 had at last enabled Bramley to receive clear pictures and, despite the initial very high cost of a set, television swept through the place. Cinema audiences began to fall until ten years after, first the Lido and then, very shortly afterwards the Clifton closed. The Lido has been demolished, the Clifton is now the home of Forest Products, a do-it-yourself centre.

Intake and Swinnow had been identified as sites for council houses as early as 1943. Yet the comparatively long period between proposal and realisation could not entirely eradicate some feeling of regret when these cultivated areas came to be built upon. Any such regret had to be set against the Council's claim that new houses were needed to replace slum properties and to counter over-crowding in other parts of Leeds. It was argued that even when such areas were cleared, and new houses built on the cleared land, there would still be a shortfall of houses which could be met only by building in other parts of Leeds. Unfortunately Bramley was chosen to be one of these parts. So whilst a few lost their livelihood and others a pleasing view, many gained improved living conditions. Admittedly too the case for urban dairying was becoming increasingly difficult to sustain as, since the thirties, dairy farmers obtained the same price for their milk wherever they lived and improved road transport enabled milk to be brought in from more distant places.

For a time it seemed as if widespread building had run out of steam but smaller and more patchy building continued (figure twenty-three).

Figure twenty-three: Houses built privately in 1959 in the Whitecote Area.

More often than not this took place on small vacant plots of land within an existing residential area.

The sixties, though, witnessed a renewed attack on the periphery with the building of more council houses in part of the Raynville area and at Gamble Hill. At these places, and in a small extension of the Swinnow estate, several multi-storey flats were built (figure

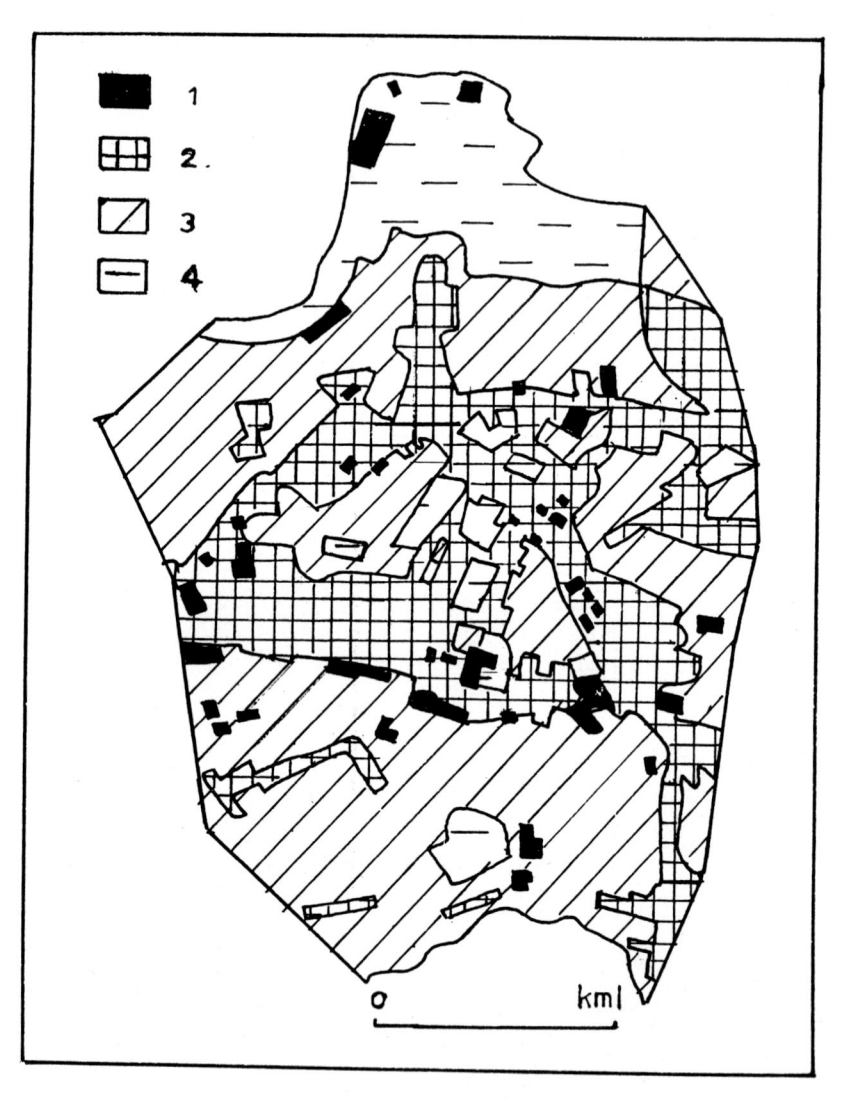

Figure twenty-four: Land Use in Bramley in 1939.
1 Manufacturing   2 Residential and Services
3 Cultivated   4 Open Land

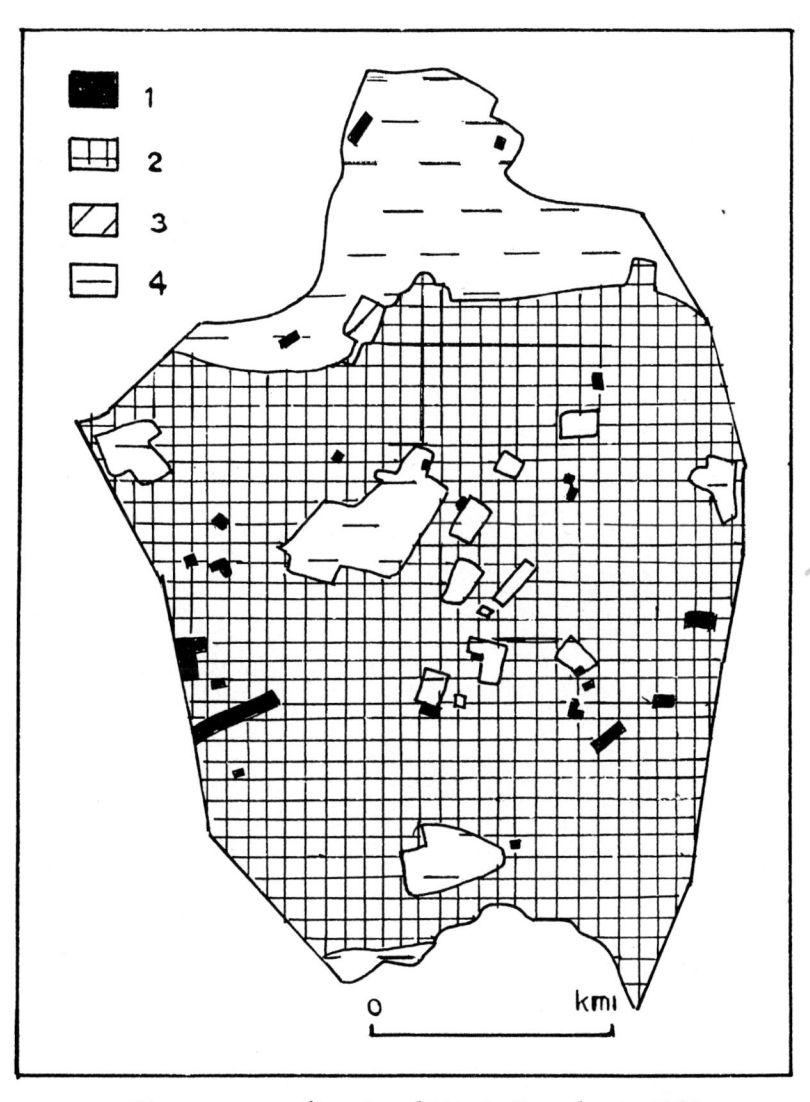

Figure twenty-five: Land Use in Bramley in 1989.
1 Manufacturing   2 Residential and Services
3 Cultivated   4 Other Open Land

Figure twenty-six: Multi-storey flats at Gamble Hill.

twenty-six). The Ducky area also succumbed to bricks and mortar though this developed as a private housing estate.

By the mid-sixties, very little cultivated land remained in the outer part of Bramley. Most of the cultivated fields had become houses and flats but a few had become recreational areas. In this way the area of Bramley Park had been substantially increased. Most, in fact, of the remaining open land was either used for outdoor recreation or was derelict land that had previously been quarried. Only at Newlay was any stone still quarried and even this quarry would shortly cease to be worked.

For some time manufacturing had been declining but it was a gradual process and some new firms, for example, Doyle and Flockton, had opened and thereby offset the losses. New localities had not developed. Instead new firms occupied either empty premises or rebuilt. Some well-known firms such as Huggan and Boyes and Helliwell had already closed but there were plenty of equally well-known firms such as Tapp and Toothill, Turner and Elmfield still in business and, in the mid-sixties, bricks, jam and soap were some of the goods still being made.

Town Street was still largely intact too, tatty perhaps, but intact nevertheless. Not only were most of the buildings those that existed in 1939 but several businesses that then existed were still operating. Witts was still printing the Weekly Advertiser, Thompsons were still baking their renowned cakes and Hamer was still selling meat. Already, though, the future was signposted in the small scale

Figure twenty-seven: Old houses prior to demolition on Granhamthorpe in 1962.

Figure twenty-eight: Granhamthorpe today.

demolition of parts of Town Street, and elsewhere as on Granhamthorpe (figure twenty-seven).

Granhamthorpe, Town Street, these streets are part of the heart of Bramley and it was this heart that now was targeted for change. As early as 1961 we had inspected plans for the future character of Town Street. We had not much cared for them but Leeds Council had already determined that Town Street must be drastically altered. All that remained to be decided was the detailed nature of the plan. Apart from the Council it is difficult to know who viewed this development with much enthusiasm. Not, one believes, those whose houses were to be demolished. Not those shop-keepers who would cease to trade and certainly not the factory workers who faced an uncertain future.

Some firms re-located. Witts and Rogers moved to Town End. Others, of which Crawshaw and Park (figure twenty-nine) is an example, closed for good. True enough their plant was dated but it is conceivable that this firm, producing very high quality worsted, would have continued for some years at least, had not the Council issued a compulsory purchase order. Simpson's dairy farm – the last in Bramley – went too (figure thirty-one). Cultivated land and factories, all were swept away by an advancing tide of housing. Most of the shops went the same way. Only the south side of Town Street between the Prospects and Broad Lane and that part of Town Street east of Barley

Figure twenty-nine: Crawshaw and Park's Mill, 1968.

Figure thirty: Near the site of Crawshaw and Park, 1989.

Figure thirty-one: Simpson's Farm 1968, almost unchanged since the mid-fifties.

Mow escaped unscathed. The replacement of shops by houses was particularly evident on the north side of Town Street between Bell Lane and Waterloo Lane (figures thirty-two and thirty-three).

Buildings were also demolished between Waterloo Lane and Outgang but on the northern side new shops were constructed (figures thirty-six and thirty-seven). As a result of these processes, shops came to be much more concentrated in this central area – "the shopping centre" – the total number of shops was much lower than in 1939 and shops and housing came to be located in much more distinct zones. Town Street looked completely different too. Brick and concrete replaced stone, flats were built and as both these and the houses were built without fireplaces there were no chimneys to diversify the skyline. Opposite the Conservative Club and in the shopping centre flat roofs were a departure from the sloping roofs of 1939. It was at this period too, that almost all the narrow old yards that led off Town Street were eradicated.

If, when old Bramley is mentioned, first thoughts go to Town Street, sight should not be lost of the very marked changes that have affected Stanningley Road between the Daisy Public House and Hough Lane. There too, many houses and shops were pulled down but, unlike Town Street, many of these sites were not rebuilt so wide areas of grass today border parts of the road.

Figure thirty-two: Town Street looking east from near the top of Bell Lane in 1971. Notice the stone buildings of varied heights and designs. The first building on the left was the Fent Shop.

Figure thirty-three: Town Street today from the same location as figure thirty-two.

Figure thirty-four: Town Street from Hough Lane and looking north, in 1975.

Figure thirty-five: Town Street today from the same location as figure thirty-four. A Council office has replaced the Midland Bank and shops.

Figure thirty-six: Central Town Street from near Outgang. The Post Office is occupying Proctor's shop in this view taken in 1971.

Figure thirty-seven: Central Town Street from near Outgang today.

Figure thirty-eight: Stanningley Road, looking west, from near its junction with Elder Road, 1951.

Figure thirty-nine: Stanningley Road today but taken from the same location as the previous photograph.

Figure forty: Yates' Wellington Mill, 1975.

Figure forty-one: The site of Yates' mill is now open land.

43

From the mid-sixties onwards jeans and other casual clothes were increasingly being worn. The home market for worsted clothing correspondingly fell and as overseas markets were also declining, it became increasingly difficult for many textile firms to survive. The closure and subsequent demolition of Elmfield took with it the mill's distinctive telescopic chimney. Yates' large Wellington Mill (figure forty) closed in 1976 with the loss of hundreds of jobs though some employees were transferred to St. Catherine's Mill and some went to Bradford. Following closure the mill was demolished and Bramley lost another landmark: Yates' hundred and fifty foot high chimney.

Detailed land use changes have also arisen through chance. When Bramley National School (figure forty-two) was burnt out it was decided to build a new school further up Hough Lane and the site of the old school has been re-developed for housing.

Figure forty-two: Bramley National School prior to re-location.

The Eighties

Following thirty years of turmoil, during which so much older property was demolished and so much cultivated land was lost to housing, it is scarcely surprising that the eighties has been a decade of relative stability. Relative because inevitably some changes have not only taken place but are still happening. The point is illustrated by Bramley shopping centre where, whilst most of its services are the same type today as in 1980, five changes had occured by the time of the survey (Appendix one) and a few have happened since. Until 1989 perhaps the greatest change in retailing, during the eighties, occured when a small shopping parade opened near the junction of Swinnow Road and Swinnow Lane. It is also in the Swinnow area that two large service developments have recently taken place. A supermarket has just opened on the site of Tapp and Toothill's works and a warehouse, built on the site of Boyes and Helliwell's mill has been re-developed as a house improvement centre.

This centre now forms part of an increasing range of services orientated towards the home. There has been a growth in the number of estate agents and solicitors, no doubt associated with the increased frequency with which houses are bought and sold. More houses now have video players and, in consequence, video libraries have sprung up in several parts of Bramley. Most of these newer services do not occupy purpose built premises, instead they have replaced shops and, sometimes houses.

In 1939 one of the delightful, but detailed, landscape features had been the works dam. The last remnants of these dams disappeared with the closure and demolition of Tapp and Toothill (figure forty-three). This firm was not the only one to close in the eighties. Engineering suffered a considerable loss when Turner's works closed. Part of the site is used by the National Steel Distributors, illustrating how service activities have increased in Bramley.

The textile industry has continued to be badly hit with the closures of Yates' St. Catherine's Mill, Ross Mills and Hill Top Mill. Most recent of all has been the closure, attributed to imports of cheap Turkish textiles, of Courtaulds' Mill. The premises, vacant for some weeks, were, for a short time, acquired by Curtain Dream but, at the time of writing, are again vacant. These currently unused premises and those of Wood's former works, at the bottom of Bath Lane, have led to gaps in the map of manufacturing.

Whilst the total area occupied by houses has not changed much, some places have shown small increases and others, small decreases.

Figure forty-three: Tapp and Toothill's dams are located on the left. In the background are the brickwork's two chimneys. On the right is Bramley station house where a fire greeted the winter traveller.

Figure forty-four: The same position from Ducky but in 1989. Safeway's supermarket car park occurs on the left. The dams, the brickworks and the old station house have all gone.

Figure forty-five: Eighties style Tudor. Intake Lane.

The process of infilling, whereby small plots of vacant land become built up, is still continuing with new houses being built at Hough Side and Intake Lane (figure forty-five). Some of those on Intake Lane are already occupied.

Re-development continues too but on a small scale. Not long ago new houses were built on the sites of demolished old houses and a factory at the eastern end of Elder Road. Structural defects have led to the demolition of some older houses in part of the Henleys thereby slightly increasing the area of open land. But it is not all old property that has been demolished. Consequent upon serious deficiencies, part of the relatively recently built Raynville estate has been demolished and here, re-building is already taking place.

There are parts of Bramley where change is now more difficult to effect than it was some twenty or more years ago. These are the parts that have been designated Conservation Areas. As its name suggests a Conservation Area is an area that is deemed desirable to preserve or enhance because it has some special historical or architectural interest. One such Area has been delineated near Hill Top but the largest Areas are approximately bounded by Broad Lane, Town Street, the Prospects, Hough Lane, Rosemont Terrace and Granhamthorpe. Included are Bramley Park, the Baths, the Unicorn, Bramley Church and a large number of stone buildings in the Warrel's area (figure forty-six).

Figure forty-six: Conservation landscape – Warrel's Grove.

    Welcome though it is that so much of old Bramley is so designated it must be conceded that the relevant Act, passed in 1967, unfortunately came too late to save other parts from destruction.

    Clearly the pace of change will be slowed in the designated areas. It is surely significant therefore that the red brick terraces of the Warrel's area are excluded from the Conservation Areas. These houses are now some of the oldest properties left and in the light of all that has happened to Bramley in the last forty years, their long-term future must be uncertain. Otherwise it seems as if, for the next few years at least, Bramley should not look much different from what it does today.

    Today cultivated land is but a shadow of its former self there being but a small area at Whitecote where some market gardening is practised. The other open land (figure twenty-five) is chiefly used for outdoor recreation including a small area devoted to allotments in the Warrel's area. Unlike fifty years ago most of Bramley is now built up. The somewhat piecemeal growth of Bramley means that it is possible, as near Coppy Lane, to see in close proximity houses of very different ages and styles. Nevertheless broad building type zones can be identified.

    Some of the newest buildings, made of brick but without chimneys (figure thirty-three) occupy the oldest part of Bramley on, and near, Town Street. As a result of the demolition of much of Town Street,

Figure forty-seven: A corner shop at the junction of Warrel's Road and Grosmont Terrace. As in 1939, it is today a confectionery shop.

many of the oldest buildings are now to be found in the Warrel's area. There most of the houses, with a few recent exceptions, fall into three types: stone built detached and semi detached (figure forty-six), stone built terraces and brick built terraces. A few corner shops still exist and a good example is shown in figure forty-seven. The continued existence of corner shops here is perhaps accounted for by the location of the Warrel's area on a plateau so a walk from the shops of the Centre, or from Stanningley Road, is uphill. Certainly the quiet and rather aloof atmosphere of fifty years ago seems to linger hereabouts. The Astons also has some old brick built terraces but these mingle with

49

Figure forty-eight: Thirties style council houses in the Fairfields.

other house styles, especially inter-war terraces. Westwards from the Warrel's lies the Fairfields which, despite some recent renovations, retains its thirties style council houses (figure forty-eight). These house styles can also be seen at Sandford. In the Calverleys and Whitecote occur one of the main areas of inter-war semi-detached private houses though some post-war houses have been added to the area (figure twenty-three). Concrete houses and flats (figure twenty-two) can be seen in the more westerly and southerly council estates, built in the immediate post-war years, at Ganners, Intake and Swinnow. As in the thirties built council estates, each of these estates has its own small parade of shops but the later constructed Gamble Hill and Raynville estates, with their multi-storey flats (figure twenty-six) were built without these little parades of shops.

The outward expansion of housing and redevelopment in the centre, have together led to the distribution of shops in 1989 being very different from fifty years ago. The distribution of butchers shops (figure forty-nine) exemplifies the location of shops today. A small concentration of shops occurs in the shopping centre, otherwise there is a scattering of butchers shops in the residential areas. The distribution of fish and chip shops (figure fifty) shows a dispersed pattern and one that is even more scattered than in 1939.

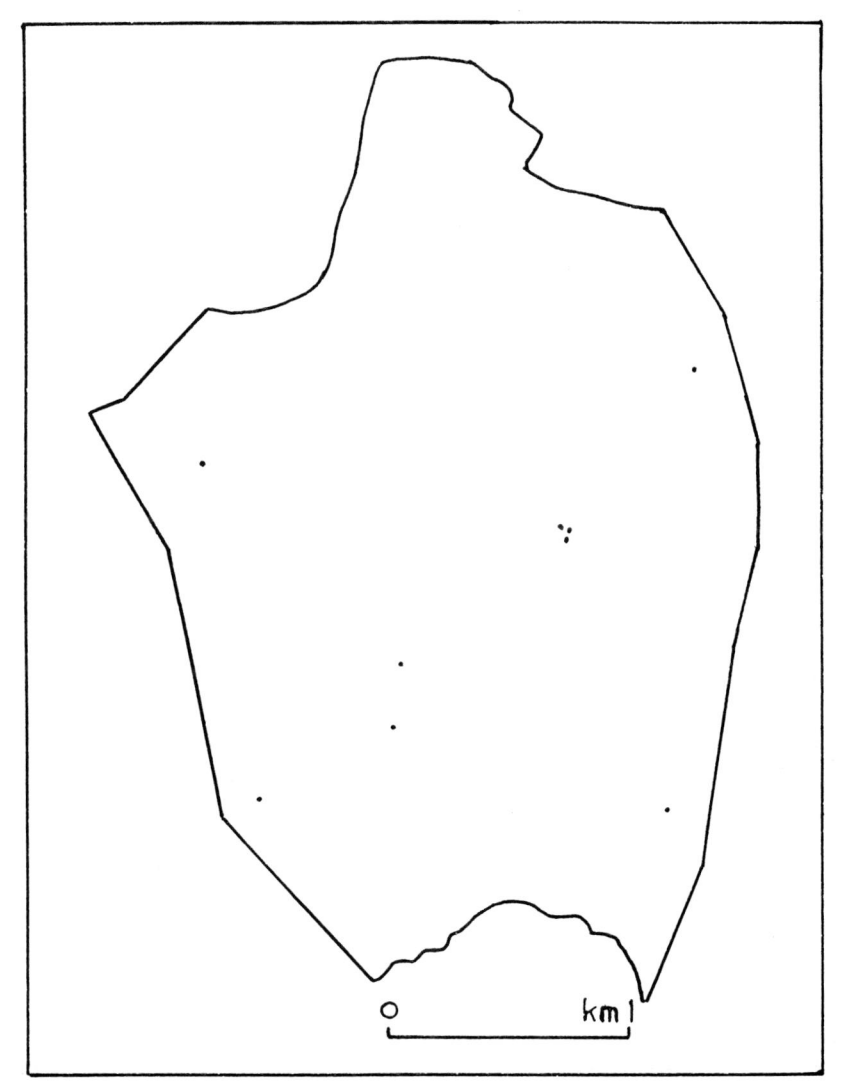

Figure forty-nine: Distribution of Butchers Shops in 1989.

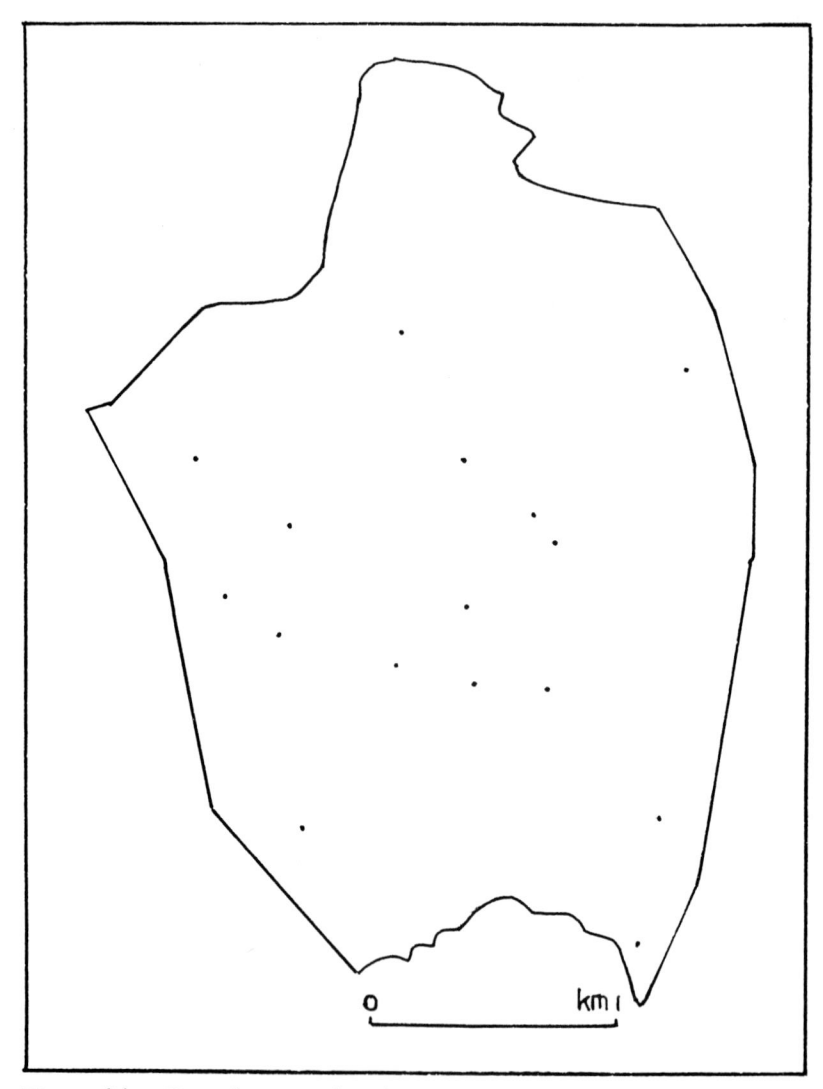

Figure fifty: Distribution of Fish and Chip Shops in 1989.

Table Three
Distribution of Shops in Bramley in 1989

Number of shops located in

	Town Street	Stanningley Road	Rest of Bramley	Total
Butchers and Greengrocers	6	2	12	20
Other food shops	11	6	47	64
Post Offices and Newsagents	2	0	17	19
Clothes and footwear	6	1	3	10
Other shops	17	5	10	32
Total	42	14	89	145

Note: Morrison's Supermarket considered as 7 units, Safeway's supermarket considered as 5 units and Swinnow Co-op considered as 3 units.

Table Four
Number of Shops in Different Parts of Town Street 1989

Broad Lane to Westover Road	Westover Road to Hough Lane	Hough Lane to Outgang	Outgang to Highfield Road	Highfield Road to Town End
5	2	34	0	1

Note Morrison's supermarket considered as 7 units.

Several interesting changes are revealed when tables one and three are compared. Despite an increase in population, the total number of shops in Bramley has decreased since 1939. The total has fallen because of a decrease in the number of food and clothes shops and so for these goods there is less competition amongst the shopkeepers and customers have less choice. Not only that, but Bramley no longer has a fishmonger and, in summer, it is now rarely possible to buy fresh raspberries and impossible to buy fresh bilberries and blackberries.

Tables one and three also show how Town Street and Stanningley Road have experienced both a relative and absolute decline as shopping districts. Shops are now more scattered throughout Bramley. Yet at a more detailed scale, a comparison of tables two and four shows that within Town Street shops have become much more markedly concentrated and that the most important area is now between Hough Lane and Outgang.

Through the closure of the bank on Stanningley Road, banks are even more clustered now than fifty years ago. A cashpoint is available at Safeways but to call in at a bank, there is no choice but to travel to the junction of Town Street, Waterloo Lane and Hough Lane as all three banks are located there. This area and an extension up Hough Lane continues to have several services. Apart from the banks, there is a solicitor, a public house, Bramley Church, a library, a school and a chapel. Overall, though, and as in 1939, non-retailing services are widely scattered through the built-up area.

One characteristic of the eighties is the sub-division of former factories into small units. Some of these are occupied by firms engaged in service provision and this has contributed towards the scattering of service activities. Manufacturing firms which occupy these units are relatively small so, whilst manufacturing has declined, there has not been a corresponding decline in the number of firms. Bramley no longer has a leather industry, and only three firms manufacturing cloth now exist: A. Brown, Croysdale-Parkland and Hanen and Ackroyd. The industries which have gained in significance are engineering, paper and printing and miscellaneous industries (Appendix two). Despite all the changes there are several interesting survivals from 1939 (Appendix three).

Occasionally a greenfield site has been developed for manufacturing, as in the case of Thurston's bakery, but, whilst some such detailed site changes have occured, no new manufacturing districts have emerged since 1939. In consequence, the differences in the distribution of manufacturing between today and fifty years ago (figures twenty-four and twenty-five) have arisen through the closure of firms and not through the development of new localities. Today there is still some manufacturing in the north but the main areas are near Bramley Town End and that part of Swinnow Lane near the Ring Road.

Today, too, with only small areas devoted to manufacturing and what there is, more concentrated, and with scarcely any cultivated land, Bramley looks much more like a typical suburb than it did fifty years ago. Yet it has achieved this character in a rather different way from that of many suburbs. Other suburbs develop largely through outward growth from a city centre. But in Bramley its suburban character has arisen through a combination of outward growth from the heart and its re-development. Economic changes, and even chance have played some part in the development of Bramley over the last fifty years. No factor, though, has been of greater significance in leading to the changes that have affected Bramley than decisions taken by Leeds City Council. So, ultimately, much of what can be seen today derives from these decisions.

And what might a child notice about Bramley today? No longer is there the smell of simmering strawberries from the jam works but at least there is the smell of baking bread from Thurstons. That, though, is almost the only relief from endless exhaust fumes. And it is the roar of the buses, lorries and aircraft that are much more likely to be heard than the rhythmic pound of looms. A really perceptive child might see some differences in house styles but those remarkably clear contrasts between farm and factory of fifty years ago are now long gone. And so too have so many of those fascinating details that would cause a child to stand and stare. No mill dams and no clanking trams. No cows either but a really diligent youngster might, even in 1989, come across a handful of sheep, watch horses grazing and discover a ruined rectangular low shed.

Just one shed but, in an older person, it might evoke the scenes of fifty years ago and, in turn, help recall the several changes that led to the landscapes of Bramley being so very different today from those of the war years.

Epilogue

Old Bramley has been demolished, cleared sites have often been rebuilt. Farms have given way to flats and houses. That sense of being part of a community, so evident before the war is, though by no means totally lost, weaker now. To some extent these changes, in landscape and community, are related. When Zion Baptist Chapel sold some of its land, lawn tennis was lost. When Brunswick and Moriah Chapels' playing fields were built upon it was no longer feasible to have cricket teams. When so many new houses were built it was almost inevitable that at least some would come to be inhabited by newcomers who lacked roots in Bramley. Now that housing is so widely spread within Bramley's confines, it is more difficult for people, resident in any one part, to feel a sense of identity with the whole.

It would be wrong, though, to relate social change solely to landscape change. Standards of living have shown a dramatic increase. In passing, we record, without comment, that politically Bramley is now a Labour stronghold. People are healthier, work fewer hours, and, as most houses are now centrally heated and have electric, or gas, ovens and washing machines, housework is easier. Most houses possess one or both of a television and video so there is now much less need to seek entertainment outside the house, and, for those who do, increased mobility has enabled people to travel well beyond Bramley.

The education system has altered too. As in the rest of Leeds, a Bramley child attends a primary school until the age of nine, a middle school from the ages of nine to thirteen and, thereafter, a high school. As a result there is less continuity in a child's education than existed several years ago. More schools now exist and they are more scattered. Perhaps because of all these changes, schools now seem far less effective in promoting, in their scholars, a sense of identity with Bramley.

People's tastes have altered so, when ballroom dancing became less fashionable, winter dances ceased to be held at the Baths. Swimming, for which a considerable demand still exists, is no longer possible in Bramley, unless one is prepared to risk a dip in the murky canal. In June, 1989 Bramley Baths closed, in order, it was stated, to effect improvements. Over a year later the building is boarded up, daily becoming decrepit and shows no sign of immediate re-opening. (May re-open 1992.) Temporary or not, the closure leaves a major gap in Bramley's recreational life. The tennis courts in Bramley Park are scarcely more useable than the Baths so perhaps we should be grateful that the Council still provides bowling facilities in the Park. There Bramley Veteran's Bowling Club is active.

Figure fifty-one: A bowling match in Bramley Park.

Whilst several social activities no longer occur in Bramley, others, like bowls, remain. The many public houses and clubs still seem to prosper, and as befits a more secular age, the shopping centre is not only the place to buy provisions but has become the spot to pass the time of day.

The role of the Church in Bramley's social life may have diminished but is by no means negligible. There is still a Bright Hour at Trinity Methodist and a Mothers Union at the Parish Church. Youngsters can join Scouts, Guides, the Girls' Brigade and the Boys' Brigade. Just as the Church as a whole now seems less visible, so too the Boys' Brigade is less heard. Those regular Sunday drum beats echoing through the streets, belong to former times. Nevertheless the Church occasionally takes the initiative in Bramley's economic and social life. Thus it was the Reverend Stonestreet who played a key part in the development of St. Catherine's Mill after it closed. For a time it seemed as if this former mill would become a permanent venue for drama and several successful productions were, in fact, staged. Unfortunately these have now ceased and the premises are the province of small industrial units. Church or chapel produced pantomimes which, for so many years, brightened Bramley's winter season have now, alas, all but ceased.

Surprisingly a carnival is still held at regular intervals. Surprising? Yes! For scarcely had the holding of a yearly carnival started again after

Figure fifty-two: Carnival 1989.

the war, than they ceased, apparently for good. However, through the efforts of Mr Heaton, and his committee, the carnival was re-instated in 1976 and it is now a biennial event. On Carnival day itself there is not only a lengthy procession of floats but a variety of other entertainment held in Bramley Park. The Carnival Committee also organises a pram race that is run every summer.

    Music and rugby have each helped to make the name of Bramley known well outside its immediate area. Bramley band, renowned though it was, is no more. Rugby still flourishes. As well as Rugby Union, which eventually found a home for itself on part of Haley's allotments in the Warrel's, Rugby League is played at Barley Mow. Most of this book was written in the first half of 1989 and, at that time, it seemed as if here, at least, was one activity that would, for many years to come, continue to exist and promote people's identity with Bramley. But towards the end of 1989 Bramley was startled to learn that the club was seeking to re-locate. Many residents voiced most strongly that Bramley Rugby Club should retain its association with the Mow.

    We do not yet know the outcome but the news seemed to re-kindle a concern for Bramley. Such concern is to be welcomed for whilst we cannot bring back the buildings and fields that have been so recently eradicated, we can at least seek to maintain the green places that remain. So let past errors strengthen our future vigilance.

Figure fifty-three: Will Bramley win?

Appendix One   Bramley Shopping Centre

Premises	Ground Level Services in 1980	1989
2	Abbey Fisheries	Centre Fish Bar
3	Smith's Racing	Smith's Racing
4	Madeley's Paint & Wallpaper	Colourvision TV and Video Sets
5	Sloan's Bread and Cakes	Sloan's Bread and Cakes[1]
6-7	Siama's Ladies Clothes	Siama's Ladies Clothes
8	Bancroft's Stationers	Bancroft's Stationers
9	Hough's Shoes and Repairs	Hough's Shoes and Repairs
10	Crockatt's Cleaners	Crockatt's Cleaners
11	Dewhurst's Butchers	Dewhurst's Butchers
12	Valdes Shoes	Barratt's Shoes
15-16	Sea Land Foods Delicatessen	Kew House Delicatessen
17	Post Office	Post Office
18	Freeman Optician	Freeman Optician
19	Howard's Jewellers	Howard's Jewellers
20	Zebedee Ladies Clothes	Zebedee Ladies Clothes
21	Kingston's Florists	Kingston's Florists
22	Morrison's Supermarket	Morrison's Supermarket
23	Leeds Permanent Building Society	Leeds Permanent Building Society
24	Steel's Butchers	Steel's Butchers
25	Bramley Apple Cafe	Bramley Apple Cafe
26	Direct Curtin Co.	Di-Mar Soft Furnishings
27	Nicholls Electric	Super Save Discount
30	Martin's Newsagents	Martin's Newsagents
31-33	Boots Chemists	Boots Chemists
34	Job Centre	Job Centre
35	Hopkinson's Chemists	Cutler's Chemists
38	Rediffusion TV Sets	Granada TV and Video Sets
39	Abbott's Bread and Cakes	Watson's Bread and Cakes
40	Shah's Ladies Shop	Boyes Travel Agent
41	Thurston's Bread and Cakes	Thurston's Bread and Cakes
42	Sugden's Hardware	Electricity Showroom
43	Co-operative Grocery	Iceland Frozen Foods
44	Former Co-operative Butcher	Bramley Carpet Centre
45	The Fruit Market	The Fruit Market
46	Keith's Fish and Chips	Fish and Chips

[1] Since the fieldwork was completed Sloan's has become Fulton's Frozen Foods

Appendix Two
Proportion of Firms in Different Types of Manufacturing

Manufacturing Type	Percentage of Firms Engaged in Manufacturing Type in	
	1939	1989
Food and Drink	5	3
Textiles	36	9
Clothing and Curtains	2	9
Wood and Furniture	11	7
Chemicals	13	2
Engineering	18	25
Paper and Plastic Containers and Printing	5	28
Miscellaneous	10	17
Total	100	100
(Total number of firms)	61	57

(Note for the 1939 figures Yates' Wellington Mill and Yates' St. Catherine Mill have been taken as two firms.)

Appendix Three
Changes to the premises of firms in manufacturing in 1939

Numbers

Firms present in 1989 at the same location as 1939

Airedale Rope Company	Calverley Lane
A. Brown Textiles	Mill Lane
Nutt Printing	Broad Lane
Walkington Furniture	Town Street
Croysdale Textiles	Stanningley Road
Town End Chemicals	Back Lane
Newsome Engineering	Elder Road
Sloan & Davidson Iron Founders	Swinnow Lane
Taylor & Atkinson Engineering	Swinnow Lane

Sub-total   9

Premises present in 1989 but have become

other manufacturing   7
    (of which one is partly derelict)

service activity   4
    (of which one is partly not in use)

sub-divided into   a) service units   5
    (of which one is partly not in use)

                   b) service and manufacturing units   4
    (of which one is partly demolished)

not in use   3

Sub-total   23

Demolished but new premises built on the site for

manufacturing	1
manufacturing and services	3
services	3
manufacturing or services but not in use	1
sub-total	8

Demolished and have now become

residential	13
derelict land	2
grassland	6
sub-total	21
Total	61

Note **included** in the above tables are firms which have re-located:

	from	to
Witts Printing	Town Street	Back Lane
Rogers Organ Pipes	Town Street	Back Lane
Battye Engineering	Hough Lane	Waterloo Lane
H. Brown Clothing	Railsford Mount	Stanningley Road
Barker Refrigerators	Elder Road	Rodley